Firstfruits
Living

Related Resources

After the publication of this book, the (Mennonite) Churchwide Stewardship Council invited Lynn Miller to serve full-time as traveling Firstfruits Teacher. During three and a half years, he spoke to more than 20,000 people in at least 250 congregations and conferences, "to provoke unto love and to good works" (Heb. 10:24, KJV).

Because of his stimulating and dramatic style, many congregations and individuals requested that a videotape of these presentations be made available. Mennonite Board of Congregational Ministries has produced this video, to enable other congregations and small groups to participate in the *Firstfruits Living* experience.

Firstfruits Living: The Video may already be in your church or conference resource center. For information on obtaining this or other videos, you may contact the distributor, Mennonite Media, 1251 Virginia Avenue, Harrisonburg, VA 22802 (1-800-999-3534).

Also by Lynn A Miller: *Just in Time: Stories of God's Extravagance.* These moving and sometimes hilarious true stories reveal the joy of firstfruits living, in which we give back the best of what an extravagant God first offered us.

The Giving Project Series

A Christian View of Money: Celebrating God's Generosity
   Mark Vincent
Teaching a Christian View of Money: Celebrating God's Generosity
   Mark Vincent
A Christian View of Hospitality: Expecting Surprises
   Michele Hershberger

Book ordering: 1-800-759-4447.

Firstfruits Living

Giving God Our Best

Foreword by
James M. Lapp

Lynn A. Miller

HERALD PRESS
Scottdale, Pennsylvania
Waterloo, Ontario

Library of Congress Cataloging-in-Publication Data
Miller, Lynn A.
    Firstfruits living : giving God our best / Lynn A. Miller.
        p. cm.
    ISBN 0-8361-3543-1 (alk. paper)
    1. Stewardship, Christian.   I. Title.
BV772.M518   1991
248´.6—dc20   90-48699

Scripture quotations are from the New American Standard Bible,
© The Lockman Foundation 1960, 1962, 1963, 1968, 1971, 1972,
1973, 1975, and are used by permission.

FIRSTFRUITS LIVING
Copyright © 1991 by Herald Press, Scottdale, Pa. 15683
    Published simultaneously in Canada by Herald Press,
    Waterloo, Ont. N2L 6H7. All rights reserved
Library of Congress Catalog Card Number: 90-48699
International Standard Book Number: 0-8361-3543-1
Printed in the United States of America
Design and cover art by Paula M. Johnson

06 05 04 03 02 01 00 99 10 9 8 7 6 5

To order or request information, please call
1-800-759-4447 (individuals); 1-800-245-7894 (trade).
Website: www.mph.org

This book is dedicated to

*The community called South Union, which has
trained more than one preacher*

*Linda, my wife, who is also a member of that
community, but with the distinct disadvantage of
having to hear everything this preacher has to say
at least twice*

*Glen and Marilyn, who looked wealth and leisure
square in the face and turned away
to walk with the poor.*

Contents

Foreword

Firstfruits is not exactly a household term. Neither is *stewardship* common parlance for most people. But talk about money and the conversation quickly generates heat if not light.

Are there fresh teachings for Christians on the subject of money that do not appeal to duty, guilt, or legalistic calculations as a way of increasing giving to the church? That is the tall order Lynn Miller set out to accomplish. In my view readers will be admirably rewarded by this small volume.

In 1985, the Mennonite Church General Assembly gave strong assent to a new ten-year vision (Vision '95) which embraces goals for growth in mission and in stewardship. The stewardship commitment of the Assembly delegates was

> to pray that personal and congregational renewal in response to God's love and generosity, even through suffering, will lead by 1995 to increasing the portion of our collective income given through congregational offerings from the present level of about 5 percent to more than 10 percent of total individual and family income.

How much movement there has been toward all

members giving a tithe through their local congregation is difficult to determine. However, as a result of this goal, giving in the church is increasing.

Lynn Miller's intention is to provide a biblical foundation for working at our vision of submitting, not only our money, but our whole lives to the purposes of God.

The study goes deeper than new techniques for raising money. Lynn probes the Scriptures for the essential character of being Christian that results in free, joyful, and generous living and giving. Firstfruits becomes a new label for "putting the kingdom first," for making God the supreme and sovereign ruler of our lives.

Combining storytelling with solid Bible study, *Firstfruits Living* calls us to examine the quality of our response to God. It invites us to respond to God's generosity with our own.

The church will be blessed by this book. Individual readers, Sunday school classes, and small groups will find here a very readable and stimulating resource for study and discussion of stewardship. Pastors may wish to develop a series of "firstfruits" sermons growing from the teaching found here.

I am pleased to commend this book. I pray that its message will stir renewal and vibrant discipleship among God's people.

—*James M. Lapp*
Executive Secretary, Mennonite
Church General Board

Author's Preface

Being asked to write a book is irresistible only once. At first, you are overwhelmed by the great honor. But after a while you begin to wonder what great sin you committed that you are now paying for. In my case, I was honored when Ray Bair called to tell me the Mennonite Church's Churchwide Stewardship Council was commissioning me to research and write a book on "firstfruits."

Firstfruits was the 1990 emphasis of the stewardship part of the 1985-1995 Ten-Year Goals for the Mennonite church. The Stewardship Council believed that renewed understanding of and commitment to firstfruits giving might be responsible for at least half of the projected doubling of per member giving. Having met me at the previous meeting, they wanted me to put that new understanding together. Who wouldn't be honored?

Committed to living out as much of the Anabaptist vision as possible, including the "community hermeneutic" (Bible interpretation in a group setting), I made the project a congregational one.

The congregation released me from pastoral care for six months and preaching for three months. The first month I retreated into my office to see just how big "firstfruits" was going to be. Then for ten weeks I studied the appropriate texts during the week.

On Sundays I brought my understandings to a class of people willing to struggle with the meaning for us today. After each class I went back to my study to turn our community interpretation into next Sunday's sermon. Thus came about community authorship!

But, much to my surprise and disappointment, a series of sermons a book does not make. It looked so easy. But now I was wondering if this assignment was simply the Stewardship Council giving me my "just deserts" for holding their collective feet to the fire at the New Carlisle meeting (see chapter 1).

The problem, it turned out, was that I thought I had discovered the secret of the universe in the term *firstfruits*. What I had on paper was too broad to interest anyone, much less inspire them to make major changes.

It wasn't until I had heard that comment from at least four important individuals and three congregations that I narrowed my sweeping scope. Then I concentrated on the most ignored part of our worship services—the offering.

Now, lo and behold, a book began to appear. The thanks I have to give go, therefore, to those who persistently prodded me toward what you are about to read:

Ray and Lillian Bair and the entire Stewardship Council, who initiated and sustained the project;

The South Union congregation, who gave up my time and some of their spiritual sanity so that this thing might come about;

Michael King of Herald Press, who, having just become an editor, cut his editorial teeth on an untried author and an obscure theme;

Arnold Roth, who risked his relationship with several Franconia conference pastors and congregations to try it out in the pews;

Marlene and Stan Kropf, who struggled with me one hot day in Fort Wayne to find an interesting and versatile structure for the book;

The Carlsbad, New Mexico, and Orrville, Ohio, congregations who each suffered through four long sessions of "how firstfruits explain the universe."

Thank you all for your patience and help. Now I understand why so much space in a book is devoted to giving thanks—there is so much to be given.

A Word to Teachers About the Design of the Book

The book is designed for small groups and classes of people committed to learning more about ways God wants us to use God's resources.

It is divided into thirteen chapters for use over an entire quarter. But by assigning the six stories as preparatory reading and the seven Bible studies for class time, you could combine this study with another six-lesson study to fill a quarter.

A companion video tape for each chapter with a storytelling introduction by the author is available (from South Union Mennonite Church, West Liberty, Ohio) for use in opening the discussion sessions.

—*Lynn Miller*
West Liberty, Ohio

1

The Trouble with Money

In 1986 a group of Mennonites involved in the stewardship ministry of the denomination gathered at New Carlisle, Ohio, for their annual meeting. Their responsibility was coordinating stewardship education and activity from coast to coast; their task for that meeting was to develop strategy for achieving next year's denominational goal of "Every Member Adopting a Modest Living Standard."

Millard Fuller, founder of Habitat for Humanity, was keynote speaker. He told of his journey from self-made, self-indulgent wealth to more modest and faithful living.

This created much discussion. It strengthened the group's resolve to lead the church toward adopting modest living standards. Mennonites have long held simple living to be a virtue almost on par with the commandments of Jesus in the Sermon on the Mount.

As spirited as the discussion was, however, it never turned very specific. A journalist charged with describing the meeting in the weekly denominational magazine wondered exactly how much in dollars and cents a "modest living standard" was. "If a living standard is the amount of money a person or a family spends on themselves and their needs," he asked, "just how much is modest?"

There was a long silence. It became clear that no one was able or willing to suggest where that upper limit might be.

The journalist persisted. "Surely we could say that spending a million dollars per year on ourselves is beyond a modest living standard."

"Oh yes! A million is far too high," laughed one person.

"Well, how about $500,000?" asked the reporter. "Can we agree that half a million is also too much for the followers of Christ?"

"Sure," someone said. "After all, considering what we make, a half a million is not much different than a million."

"Okay," said the now less-frustrated journalist. "How about $100,000?"

Suddenly, as if the trigger of a fire extinguisher had been pulled, the flames of enthusiasm for defining modest living standards diminished.

"You can't make that judgment for other people," one person said.

"It depends on where you live," said another. "After all, what is modest for one may not be for another," he explained.

"But surely," the journalist persisted, "we as the church can speak to the church in very specific terms about how much is too much."

"Oh no," insisted the protester. "It's up to each person. It's a private matter, a matter between each Christian and God."

I was the journalist at that meeting. I remember coming to two tentative and disturbing conclusions following the discussion. First, most of the people at that meeting probably hoped someday to have a living standard somewhere around $100,000 per year. Second, money was one of the more difficult things to talk about in the church.

Since that time I have come to know personally many of the people present at that meeting and have discarded my first tentative conclusion. But the second tentative conclusion has become firm.

Once there were three things that were so private that you couldn't discuss them in the church. Death. Sex. And money. But being open about the realities of death has become almost mandatory in the church. And sex has become the hot topic (no pun intended) in peer groups. Money, however, continues to be the one forbidden topic.

At a recent regional conference an announcement was made concerning an upcoming financial-planning seminar for members of local congregations. This seminar would discuss budgets, investments, estates, and giving practices.

As an aside, the person giving the announcement said that the average giving of that denomination's members was about five and a half percent of net income. During the open-mike time immediately following, a woman came to the microphone. She spoke in an agitated and angry tone.

"You people," she said, "sound like you know what I make and what I give. That is nobody's business except mine and the Lord's."

This strong sense of privacy about both our incomes and giving practices is alive and strong in the religious community of North America. Few topics raise as much emotion in church settings as does the topic of money—money made and money given. Everyone seems sensitive, whether rich or poor, and nobody wants it known that they belong in either financial category.

The study of firstfruits is much more than a study of our attitudes toward money and the Sunday morning offering. But it may not be possible to study firstfruits if we don't begin by looking at our current attitudes toward money. Perhaps the best way to begin is by telling the story of the crab.

One of the more amazing things about God's creative genius in the animal kingdom is *bilateral symmetry*. For most animals, the right side of the body is almost a mirror image of the left side. If you think about it, that seems obvious. Bilateral symmetry is easy to see in humans. The right arm and right leg are usually mirror images of the left arm and left leg. The right side of the mouth and the right eye are almost identical to the left side of the mouth and the left eye, and so on. Although it may be less obvious, the same is true for most animals.

But this is not universally true. There are a few exceptions, including the crab. For some reason, the crab is one of the few creatures that is bilaterally asymmetrical. One side is different than the other. Some crabs have one large claw and one small claw, very handy when it comes to gathering food. The small claw is for close work and the larger one for work at a distance. One wonders why God did not create more animals with this clever design.

Now crabs are generally known to be greedy. But there was this one crab who was not merely greedy. He was excessively and aggressively greedy. And this crab had developed a certain tenacity to go along with his greediness. He would grab anything that looked like food with his large or small claw and never let go until it was dead and ready to be eaten. This crab prided himself on his ability to hang on to almost anything.

One day, a shadow passed over the crab's home on the bottom of the sea. It was a fishing boat towing a large net across the bottom. A few minutes after the boat had passed overhead, the net went by on the bottom. It churned up the silt and the mud and generally made a mess of things.

But, as we all know, in every mess there is an opportunity just waiting to be seized. Our crab quickly saw this opportunity. With all the mud and silt stirred up in the water, visibility was down to nothing. This would be a good time for a hungry crab to go hunting. No telling what tasty morsel one might sneak up on in all that murk.

Our aggressive and tenacious crab left his little home and cast about in the cloudy water with his large claw. Sure enough, in a few minutes he spotted something moving around in the gloom. Quick as a flash, he reached out, grabbed it with his smaller claw, and held on for dear life.

Unfortunately, what he had grabbed turned out to be his own larger claw, so far out in front he had mistaken it for something else. But being true to his tenacious nature, the crab refused to let go of even his own claw.

Just before the crab died of starvation, he turned his eyes up toward the God who had created him, and cursed God for his predicament.

God, observing this little drama from the throne, said to himself, "Silly crab, but it just goes to show you. Even crabs would benefit by taking a good look at what they are holding on to so tightly."

Questions to Ponder

1. How much income would be too much for you?

2. Are you willing to discuss how much money you make? Why or why not?

3. What makes the things you can't give up so important? Why is it so hard to let go of them?

4. Do you more often feel a sense of sacrifice, or joy, when you put your offering in the plate? How do you explain the difference?

2

A Sign of Ownership

The idea of making an offering to God is not a modern one. Genesis 4 says this:

> So it came about in the course of time that Cain brought an offering to the Lord of the fruit of the ground. And Abel, on his part also brought of the firstlings of his flock and of their fat portions. And the Lord had regard for Abel and his offering; but for Cain and his offering He had no regard (Genesis 4:3-5a).

Along with this early appearance of the offering comes the idea that an offering to the Lord is different from other offerings. This difference is most often captured by the term *firstfruits*.

In English Bibles, many different combinations of words are used to talk about the idea of firstfruits. These include firstborn, firstlings, first of the harvest, first shearing, the first dough, and, of course, firstfruits itself.

Those English words come from eighteen Hebrew

words and thirteen Greek words. In this chapter we will look for the origins of the concept of firstfruits.

We begin with the Hebrew words used in the Old Testament. The most common word is *bekur*. *Bekur* is a primitive Hebrew word which does not appear to have come from some other word. It is the original word and means, in its verb form, "to bear new fruit."

The Bible uses *bekur* in its first reference to things that are first—the sacrifice of the firstlings of the flock which Abel brought to the Lord in the earliest offering. Here is our first interesting learning. Firstfruits means more than fruit. It has to do with anything that is first. It does not matter whether the item is animal, vegetable, or for that matter, human. If it is the first one born, harvested, or picked, it is a firstfruit.

We do not hear of firstlings or firstfruits again until Exodus 4:22-23. Here the Lord tells Moses what God will do to Egypt to bring about the Exodus. *Bekur* is first used by the Lord to describe all of Israel as "My son, My first-born." Then it refers to the son of Pharaoh, "your first-born."

> Then you shall say to Pharaoh, "Thus says the Lord, 'Israel is My son, My first-born [my bekur]. So I said to you, "Let My son go, that he may serve Me"; but you have refused to let him go. Behold, I will kill your son, your first-born.' "

And Exodus 12:29 describes what indeed happened.

> Now it came about at midnight that the Lord struck all the first-born in the land of Egypt, from the first-born of Pha-

raoh who sat on his throne to the first-born of the captive who was in the dungeon, and all the first-born of cattle. And Pharaoh arose in the night, he and all his servants and all the Egyptians; and there was a great cry in Egypt, for there was no home where there was not someone dead.

What God had said, God did!

In Exodus 13, the concept of firstfruits is strengthened by the introduction of a new word for things that are first: *peter*. *Peter* means that which opens something; it comes from *patar*, which means "to separate."

Listen to how *peter* strengthens *bekur*. "Sanctify to Me every first-born [bekur], the first offspring [peter] of every womb among the sons of Israel, both of man and beast, it belongs to Me" (13:2). It belongs to me! Interesting. When *bekur* is strengthened by adding *peter*, a new meaning emerges. Now it refers to a strong sense of ownership—". . . it belongs to me."

Listen to Numbers 3:12-13:

Now, behold, I have taken the Levites from among the sons of Israel instead of every first-born [bekur], the first issue of the womb [peter] among the sons of Israel. So the Levites shall be Mine. For all the first-born [bekur] are Mine, on the day that I struck down all the first-born in the land of Egypt, I sanctified to myself all the first-born in Israel, from man to beast, they shall be Mine, I am the Lord.

Firstfruits are now defined by God, not so much as a matter of timing (that which was produced first), as of ownership. "It is mine!" From the day when the Lord struck down the firstborn in Egypt, all the firstborn have belonged to God.

"They are mine," God says. God has laid claim to the firstborn, the firstfruits. And God, of course, has a right to that claim. God created all that is; surely God can claim a portion, even the first portion.

Not only does God exercise the claim, God guards it jealously. Listen to how jealous God is of this portion, the firstfruit.

> Now it shall come about when the Lord brings you to the land of the Canaanite, as He swore to you and to your fathers, and gives it to you, that you shall devote to the Lord the first offspring [peter] of every womb, and the first offspring of every beast that you own, the males belong to the Lord. But every first offspring of a donkey you shall redeem with a lamb . . . and every first-born of man among your sons you shall redeem (Exodus 13:11-12).

Here is a new thought—that the people must redeem the firstfruits from the ownership of the Lord. The word *redeem* means to purchase. The Israelites wanted to buy the firstborn of their draft animals and their children from the Lord. That makes sense, since the Lord not only owns them in the first place, but guards that ownership zealously. If the firstborn of a donkey was not redeemed, the people were to break its neck. They were not allowed to possess the firstfruits if they had not been redeemed.

Redemption is what Mary and Joseph were up to when they took Jesus to the temple and gave an offering.

And when the days for their purification according to the law of Moses were completed, they brought Him up to Jerusalem to present Him to the Lord, (as it is written in the Law of the Lord, "Every first-born male that opens the womb shall be called holy to the Lord"), and to offer a sacrifice according to what was said in the Law of the Lord, "A pair of turtledoves or two young pigeons" (Luke 2:22-24).

Mary and Joseph redeem this firstborn son who belongs to the Lord.

Perhaps that is why in Genesis 4 the Lord was not pleased with Cain or his sacrifice. Perhaps it was not the first of Cain's harvest as Abel's was. And if not, then the Lord was displeased because Cain had kept for himself what belonged to God, merely giving the Lord some of the harvest.

Everything that belongs to the Lord is off-limits for Israel because it is holy. And every firstborn, the first offspring of both person and beast, belongs to the Lord. If the people do not buy or redeem the firstborns from the Lord, they may not use them.

So how do you redeem the firstborn? Let's go back to Exodus 12.

Then Moses called for all the elders of Israel, and said to them, "Go and take for yourselves lambs according to your families, and slay the Passover lamb. And you shall take a bunch of hyssop and dip it in the blood which is in the basin, and apply some of the blood that is in the basin to the lintel and the two doorposts; and none of you shall go outside the door of his house until morning.
"For the Lord will pass through to smite the Egyptians;

and when He sees the blood on the lintel and on the two
doorposts, the Lord will pass over the door and will not
allow the destroyer to come in to your houses to smite
you" (vv. 21-23).

The people of Israel are God's firstborn nation.
They are redeemed by taking a lamb, sacrificing it, and
putting some of its blood on both doorposts and on
the lintel above the door. And the Lord passed over
every house that had lamb's blood on the doorposts
and the lintel.

But the Lord killed all the firstborn of Egypt, both
cattle and human, for they were not redeemed by the
blood of the lamb. "The blood of the lamb." Now
where have we heard that expression before?

> Knowing that you were not redeemed with perishable
> things like silver or gold from your futile way of life in-
> herited from your forefathers, but with precious blood, as
> of a lamb unblemished and spotless, the blood of Christ
> (1 Peter 1:18-19).

> And when He had taken the book, the four living crea-
> tures and the twenty-four elders fell down before the
> Lamb . . . And they sang a new song, saying, "Worthy art
> Thou to take the book, and break its seals, for Thou wast
> slain, and didst purchase for God with Thy blood men
> from every tribe and tongue and people and nation"
> (Revelation 5:8-9).

> But when Christ appeared as a high priest of the good
> things to come, He entered through the greater and more
> perfect tabernacle, not made with hands, that is to say, not
> of this creation; and not through the blood of goats and

calves, but through His own blood, He entered the holy place, once for all, having obtained eternal redemption (Hebrews 9:11-12).

We have been redeemed by the blood of the lamb, just as Israel was. Israel was redeemed from slavery in Egypt; we are redeemed from slavery to sin. The principle is the same. Only the lamb has changed. Instead of the offspring of a sheep or a goat, a spotless animal without blemish or defect, now it is Christ, the blemish-free, sinless, firstborn of God.

James says that "in the exercise of His will He brought us forth by the word of truth, so that we might be, as it were, a certain kind of first fruits among His creatures" (1:18). We are therefore a firstfruits offering from God to the rest of creation. We are that special offering because, and only because, we have been redeemed by the blood of the Lamb of God.

Questions to Ponder

1. Abel raised food. What do you raise or make or produce? Houses? Medical services? Profits? Homemaking duties?

2. Depending on what you produce, what would it mean to give God the firstfruits?

3. If we ourselves are a firstfruits offering from God to the rest of creation, how does this affect our willingness to give God our own firstfruits?

3

The
$21.73

A few years ago, I was invited to attend the annual Mennonite Voluntary Service Retreat held near Kansas City. During the retreat worship times, many VSers shared stories of faith from their service experiences.

At one point, Tim Stuckey, serving in Tucson, Arizona, told us about the unit there. It consists of two full-time carpenters and several winter-season volunteers. The task of the unit is to provide basic home-repair services to families that are too poor to hire such help.

In Tucson, this service unit has become well known as a place of last resort for the poor. The city's social-service agencies know that if carpentry, plumbing, or electrical help is not available anywhere else, this small group of volunteers can be counted on to do something.

And so it was that a city caseworker called Tim and told him of a family that needed help. This family had managed over the years to save $400 to hire a local contractor to build one small bedroom on the side of their extremely small house.

The contractor agreed to build the room for the $400. He came one day and dug a small foundation ditch, poured a concrete footer next morning, then delivered and dumped a truckload of sand. He collected the $400 and promptly disappeared, never to be heard from again. No contractor, no room, no $400.

When Tim went to the house, he found that the family consisted of a woman named Lupita; her three young children Valentine, George, and Elizabeth; and her mother, Virginia. In the poorer sections of Tucson there are a lot of families like that, families of women and children covering three or more generations.

What made this family special was that Lupita, the mother of the children, had multiple sclerosis. The disease was slowly and painfully taking over her nervous system. When the contractor stole their $400, Lupita was completely bedfast.

To make matters worse, for this household of five there were only two rooms—a kitchen and another room that at night became a bedroom for the entire family. The children curled up in the one bed with their crippled mother; the grandmother, Virginia, slept on the floor beside the bed. It is not hard to understand why they wanted to build another room.

Tim and another volunteer Ralph Stutzman didn't need much convincing to finish building the room the contractor had started. Then they went ahead and built another one right beside it. Now, besides the living room, in which Lupita slept and lived, and the kitchen, there was a bedroom for her mother, Virginia, and a bedroom for the three children. And because of their involvement with the family, Tim and Ralph became sort of uncles for the children and good friends of Lupita and Virginia.

Some time after they had finished the building project, Tim and Ralph dropped in on the family. While Ralph was talking to Lupita and the children, Virginia quietly motioned for Tim to follow her to the kitchen. When they were alone, Virginia reached into the cupboard and brought down a small brown paper bag.

She gave the bag to Tim and told him that for the past months, since the rooms had been built, she had been saving dollar bills in the bag. The children had added 73 cents in change that they had earned or found. Then she told Tim that this $21.73 was an offering to the work of the Lord, work Tim and Ralph were doing.

At first Tim refused to take the bag and the $21.73 and tried to give it back to Virginia. But she wouldn't take it. Then Tim made sure she understood that the Voluntary Service workers couldn't take payment for what they had done.

Virginia said, "The money is not payment for what you and Ralph did but a gift to the Lord."

"I'm sure you and Lupita and the children really need the money," Tim said.

"What we really need is to return something to God in thanks for the love God showed us," Virginia answered.

Tim finally understood. He took the bag. On the following Sunday, he put the $21.73 in the offering plate on behalf of Virginia, Lupita, Valentine, George, and Elizabeth.

Questions to Ponder

1. How might God feel about that $21.73? Has anyone ever given you something you did not really need—but which they needed to give to you?

2. How do you know someone is "in love" with, or allied with you? Think of your loyalties—in marriage, at work, at the national level. How do other people know you are loyal to them? How does a gift express loyalty? How might an offering show loyalty?

4

A Sign of the Covenant

Can you believe it? Some people actually think that there is no humor in the Bible. The Bible is chock full of humor, specifically in the form of good-news/bad-news jokes. God delights in giving us what might be called "mixed blessings," good news mixed with apparent bad news.

The original good news is in Genesis 1:29. God blessed Adam and Eve and said to them, "Behold, I have given you every plant yielding seed that is on the surface of all the earth, and every tree which has fruit yielding seed, it shall be food for you." And in Genesis 2:16 the Lord God said to the human, "From any tree of the garden you may eat freely."

That's good news! Genesis 2:17 then gives the bad news: "But from the tree of the knowledge of good and evil you shall not eat." The good news was that people could eat from almost every plant on earth. The bad news was that there was an exception—they could eat everything except what they most wanted to eat.

Here is more good/bad news. All through the time known as the Exodus, God gave the people the good news that the Promised Land was waiting for them on the other side of the Jordan. In Leviticus 25:1-2, the Lord speaks to Moses at Mount Sinai and affirms the good news. "Speak to the sons of Israel and say to them, 'When you come into the land which I shall give you. . . .' "

But in verse 23, God lowers the boom and tells the bad news. God says, "The land, moreover, shall not be sold permanently, for the land is Mine, for you are but aliens and sojourners with Me." Good news: I am going to give you the land. Bad news: it really isn't going to be yours.

In Numbers 18, God tells Aaron, the high priest, the good news that God has given to Aaron and the Levites all the gifts, sacrifices, and offerings given to the Lord. And not just any old gifts either. These gifts are firstfruits. "All the best of the fresh oil and all the best of the fresh wine and of the grain, the firstfruits of those which they give to the Lord, I give them to you" (v. 12).

According to verse 16, they get the five shekels of silver which is the redemption price of every firstborn son. In verses 17-18, they get the meat from goats and oxen. And verse 19 summarizes the Lord's good news to Aaron and the Levites: "All the offerings of the holy gifts, which the sons of Israel offer to the Lord, I have given to you and your sons and your daughters with you, as a perpetual allotment. It is an everlasting covenant of salt before the Lord to you and your descendants with you."

But verse 20 gives the bad news: "The Lord said to Aaron, 'You shall have no inheritance in their land, nor own any portion among them.' " The good news is that the Levites will get all the gifts and offerings and sacrifices that come to God. The bad news is that they will need them, because they don't get a share of the promised land.

God has made unusual arrangements for the Levites, but that should not surprise us. For the Levites are a special people for God.

> Again the Lord spoke to Moses, saying, "Now, behold, I have taken the Levites from among the sons of Israel instead of every first-born, the first issue of the womb among the sons of Israel. So the Levites shall be Mine. For all the first-born . . . in the land of Egypt, I sanctified to Myself all the first-born in Israel, from man to beast. They shall be Mine; I am the Lord" (Numbers 3:11-13).

Again we see the firstfruits principle of God's exclusive ownership of the firstborn, as God redeems all Israel's firstborn by taking all Levites.

This is not simply some nice but fuzzy concept. It reflects a careful formula, correct mathematically as well as conceptually. In Numbers 3:39-51, the Lord trades the firstborn of Israel, all 22,273 of them, for all the Levites, 22,000.

And the Lord takes 1,365 shekels of silver in change to even out the bargain. The Lord is not about to let those extra 273 firstborn sons of Israel pass by as some sort of divine tip. This Lord not only wants the Levites, God wants change for the 273, and in silver!

Now surely a Lord this careful about keeping things

even is not going to let the Levites down when it comes to being landless. As we have already seen, not only do they get all the gifts and sacrifices and offerings, but also God's own very personal gift. "Then the Lord said to Aaron, 'You shall have no inheritance in their land, nor own any portion among them; I am your portion and your inheritance among the sons of Israel' " (Numbers 18:20).

Now, so we don't get the idea that the Levites have become little gods, in verse 26 the Lord makes it clear that they, too, are expected to worship God with their offerings and offer their own tithe of the tithe. If we think about it, that is what pastors' offerings are—a tithe of a tithe—for they are paid from the offerings.

In addition, the Lord offers the Levites something to take the place of land. They are given cities and pasture lands by the other tribes (Numbers 35:1-3).

When the land of Canaan was divided up among the tribes, at first the tribe of Levi was left out (Joshua 13:14). But then the sons of Israel gave the Levites cities to live in and pasture lands around the cities (Numbers 35:1-3). Then why did they need all of the firstfruits, the gifts and offerings and sacrifices?

Maybe the Levites didn't need the firstfruits as much as we thought they did. That brings us to this chapter's first point about firstfruits. Firstfruits are not a matter of need or practical economics. God certainly doesn't need the meat or the grain, and perhaps the Levites don't really need them either. Firstfruits, you see, are not a matter of need; they are a matter of worship.

Firstfruits don't have to make sense economically;

they make sense spiritually. The firstfruits offering is given to God because it belongs to God. The firstfruits offering is a constant reminder to us that God is creator and ultimate owner of all that is, and God controls all that is.

Combining what we learned earlier about the firstfruits offering, we can now say that the firstfruits offering is not a matter of timing or economics. It is a matter of ownership and worship.

Now maybe that is not such bad news at all. Maybe this is not a good-news/bad-news joke; maybe it is a good-news/good-news joke. The good news is that God has chosen the Levites as God's servants and has given them all the offerings and gifts and sacrifices. And the good news is that God will be their inheritance as well. The good news is that they will be God's. And the good news is that God will be theirs.

That leads us to the second point of this chapter— the principle of firstfruits goes both ways. The Levites become the firstfruits of God; now God is theirs. God is not only the creator, God is steward of what God has created. Two sides of a divine covenant: "They are my possession, I will be their possession."

But that was back then, before Christ. And since the old covenant foreshadows what is to come in the new covenant, what actually has come? How has the purpose of the lamb of the Passover been fulfilled? How has the purpose of the Levites been fulfilled?

Listen to these Scriptures about the fulfillment of the Levites.

He has made us to be a kingdom, priests to His God and Father (Revelation 1:6).

And Thou hast made them to be a kingdom and priests to our God; and they will reign upon the earth (Revelation 5:10).

You also, as living stones, are being built up as a spiritual house for a holy priesthood, to offer up spiritual sacrifices acceptable to God through Jesus Christ (1 Peter 2:5).

You are a chosen race, a royal priesthood, a holy nation, a people for God's own possession, that you may proclaim the excellencies of Him who has called you out of darkness into His marvelous light; for you once were not a people, but now you are the people of God; you had not received mercy, but now you have received mercy (1 Peter 2:9-10).

Christians are chosen, a priesthood, a holy nation, a people for God's own possession.

Chosen: We are indeed a chosen people, for we have been chosen to be the firstfruits of God. We belong to God.

A royal priesthood: Like Aaron and the Levites, our role is not simply to live like all the other tribes on the earth, passing down land and property from generation to generation. We are to be different from the others, just like the Levitical priesthood of old was different from the other tribes. God will be our inheritance; God will be our property.

A holy nation: As Christians we are a holy nation. The word holy here is *hagios*, meaning "the sacred ones"—not profane or common or part of the crowd, but sacred and holy. We are that part which belongs to God. The firstfruits are holy and sacred, and we are that holy and sacred part.

A people for God's own possession: The word *possession*

has roots which mean "to preserve, to keep from decay." We are kept by the God who takes good care of the divine property.

This is no good-news/bad-news joke. This is all good news. We are God's. We are not Satan's or America's or the earth's; we are God's.

And God is ours. Land is not ours, houses are not ours, things are not ours—God is ours. Good news and good news: we are God's and God is ours.

Questions to Ponder

1. How do you view the Sunday morning offering? Is it a necessary evil that pays for the working of the church? Or is it a sacrament, a matter of worship?

2. How might your congregation's observance of the offering be changed to make it more of a celebrative sacrament—a matter of giving to God what belongs to God?

5

Dreams Dreamed and Visions Seen

Once a man learned he had an incurable disease. The news filled him with great fear and sadness, for he had dreamed dreams and seen visions. Now it seemed that they would never come true. One day he heard there was a God who could do wonderful things for people, so he decided to visit this God.

"What is it you want?" asked God.

"I have dreamed dreams and seen visions, but now I am to die," replied the man.

"Tell me, what is it you have dreamed, and what are your visions?" asked the Lord God.

"I have dreamed of a home, a home of my own to live in. A big home with many rooms and fine furniture."

"You only had to ask," said the Lord. With a snap of the fingers, God created a beautiful home. Nay, a castle! The castle was far bigger, far more beautiful than the man had ever dreamed of. There were too many rooms to count, each filled with exquisite furniture.

Full of joy, the man entered the house of his dreams. He walked its halls and explored its rooms.

But before he could finish visiting all of the rooms in the castle, he felt faint from exertion and remembered his incurable disease. Again he was filled with great fear and sadness. He returned to God.

"What is it you want of me?" God asked.

"I have dreamed dreams and seen visions, but I am still going to die," said the man.

"What have you dreamed?"

"I have dreamed of food, food fit for a king. Food that would fill all my desires, food as I have never eaten before."

"You only had to ask," said God.

God snapped his fingers. At once the castle table was covered with fine and delicious food. Never had the man seen such food or tasted such goodness. It was food fit for a hundred kings. He was filled with joy as he sat at the banquet table.

But then, even before he could finish tasting all the food, he felt queasy. He remembered the incurable sickness, and the sadness and fear came upon him again. He returned to God.

"What is it you want of me?" God asked.

"I have dreamed dreams and seen visions," the man replied. "But my illness still fills me with fear and sadness."

"Tell me what have you dreamed."

"I have dreamed of clothes, fine, rich, and beautiful clothes."

"You only have to ask," said God.

With a snap of God's fingers, the man was clothed in

the finest clothes he had ever seen. His castle was filled with clothes, rich and beautiful clothes of the finest cloth imaginable.

The man walked through his magnificent castle in his exquisite clothes. He sat at his banquet table still filled with the finest food. And he was filled with happiness.

But then, when he was admiring his image in a sparkling silver goblet on the table, he noticed that the color of his clothes made his skin look even paler than before, and he remembered his disease. The sadness and fear overcame him again.

"Why are you still sad and fearful?" asked God. "Have I not fulfilled your every dream and vision? Do you not have a castle, and clothes, and fine food just as you wished? What more could you want?"

"To be cured from this illness," said the man. "Then I would be truly happy. Will you give me that?"

"No," said God. "I'm sorry, I can't give you that. But I can give you one more thing that is better than that."

"What could be better than to be cured from a fatal disease?" asked the man.

"I too, have dreamed dreams and had visions," replied God. "What I can give you is my dream, my vision."

"Will that make me happy in spite of my disease?" asked the man.

"Very happy indeed," God said.

"Then give me your dream and your vision," said the man.

"You only had to ask," said God. Another snap of the fingers and there was Jesus. Standing on the shattered remains of a broken cross, in front of an open and empty tomb, there was Jesus, alive and well and smiling.

After a moment, the man also smiled; then he turned and walked away. Away from the castle of stone, away from the food and the exquisite clothes. The man walked away from them all as if they were nothing, which they were compared to the happiness that now flooded his soul.

He still had the disease, but he was happier than he had ever dreamed. He was happier than he had ever been in his entire life, for he had seen a dream and a vision that went beyond life itself.

He was that happy the rest of his days. And he truly lived until he died.

(This is my retelling of John Aurelio's "The Parable," in *Story Sunday*, Paulist Press, 1978.)

Questions to Ponder

1. Why does seeing beyond ordinary life make some people different?

2. What vision or dream would you have to see to change your life?

3. What "firstfruits offering" could God give that might have this effect on you?

6

Christ, God's Firstfruit Offering for Us

The central teaching of the earliest apostles about Jesus Christ was his bodily resurrection. "He lives, he lives, Christ Jesus lives today." These beginning words in the refrain of a popular Easter gospel song form the central tenet of the apostles' message.

The resurrection of Christ was the core of everything those witnesses taught. In fact, the earliest job description of an apostle was simply to be a witness to Jesus' resurrection. When the eleven remaining disciples were trying to decide who would replace Judas, they talked about that person's qualifications and the task of being an apostle.

> It is therefore necessary that of the men who have accompanied us all the time that the Lord Jesus went in and out among us—beginning with the baptism of John, until the day that He was taken up from us—one of these should become a witness with us of His resurrection (Acts 1:21-22).

Now that Jesus was gone, their task was to be witnesses of his resurrection. In that first speech to the assembled crowd in Jerusalem on the day of Pentecost, Peter again and again referred to the resurrection of Jesus.

> This Man, delivered up by the predetermined plan and foreknowledge of God, you nailed to a cross by the hands of godless men and put Him to death. And God raised Him up again, putting an end to the agony of death, since it was impossible for Him to be held in its power (Acts 2:23-24).

Later, speaking from the prophecy of David about the Christ who was to come, Peter

> looked ahead and spoke of the resurrection of the Christ, that He was neither abandoned to Hades, nor did his flesh suffer decay. This Jesus God raised up again, to which we are all witnesses (vv. 31-32).

When the beggar in front of the temple was healed of his lameness, Peter told the bystanders,

> But you disowned the Holy and Righteous One, and asked for a murderer to be granted to you, but put to death the Prince of life, the one whom God raised from the dead—a fact to which we are witnesses (Acts 3:14-15).

And again, when Peter and the rest were ordered by the Sanhedrin to not continue teaching in the name of Jesus, they answered,

We must obey God rather than men. The God of our fathers raised up Jesus, whom you had put to death by hanging Him on a cross. He is the one whom God exalted to His right hand as a Prince and a Savior, to grant repentance to Israel and forgiveness of sin. And we are witnesses of these things (Acts 5:29-32a).

The message is plain. God raised Jesus from the dead, and we now witness to what God has done. We are witnesses to the resurrection, and that is our central message.

I am amazed, however, at the number of Christians who don't believe in the bodily resurrection of Jesus Christ. I keep meeting people who believe in God; they believe that Jesus lived as a real man and died a real death. But they don't believe he was really raised from the dead.

That doesn't make any sense to me. If you believe in God, why not believe in the bodily resurrection of Jesus?

Part of the problem may come from our modern conception of history. Ernst Troeltsch, a nineteenth-century German philosopher, stated what he called his three principles of history. These principles said that you can only believe that something actually happened (is historical), if it (1) has happened before, (2) is very similar to something that has happened before, and (3) has some readily apparent cause—and even then you can't be absolutely sure.

When I ask people today who don't believe in the resurrection of Christ why they don't believe, I often get a variation of one of these Troeltsch-ian axioms. "It has never happened before. It's not like anything that has ever happened before." Or, "There is no reasonable explanation for how it happened."

But God (1) has never happened before, (2) is not in the least bit similar to anything that has ever happened before, and (3) has no apparent cause or reasonable explanation. Why would someone who believes in this God not also believe in the resurrection of Jesus Christ?

Jesus was the son of God, both fully God and fully man (which also has never happened before, is not like anything that has ever happened before, and has absolutely no reasonable explanation or cause). Why would someone who believes this deny that God raised Jesus from the dead?

I wonder if one obstacle is simply pride. We want to be known as wise people. More importantly, we want to be known as people who are right about most things. We want to hold the right opinions.

Are we so afraid of being seen as gullible people, willing to believe things that are naturally impossible, that we would deny this central tenet of Christian faith? Is it possible that we doubt the resurrection because we think it is not mature to believe in it?

People who do not believe miracles such as the resurrection of the dead are not new on the face of the earth. As Peter and the others were speaking to the people and the priests (Acts 4), the Sadducees came upon them. They were greatly disturbed because the Christians were teaching the people and "proclaiming in Jesus the resurrection from the dead" (v. 2).

Notice that instead of just proclaiming that Jesus was raised from the dead, the apostles were preaching that everyone would be raised from the dead. They were proclaiming, in Jesus, the resurrection of the dead. In terms of resurrection, they had moved from the specific—Jesus, to the general—everyone.

When Paul was brought before the governor, he argued that he did serve the God of the fathers,

> believing everything that is in accordance with the Law, and that is written in the Prophets; having a hope in God, which these men cherish themselves, that there shall certainly be a resurrection of both the righteous and the wicked (Acts 24:14-15).

Now we have it. Not only was Jesus raised from the dead, all will be raised. In Acts 24:21, Paul comes right out with it: "For the resurrection of the dead I am on trial before you today."

Paul had good reason to believe he was being tried for his insistence on the resurrection of the dead. Sometime after he came back from his first visit to Corinth, Paul wrote a letter to the church at Corinth to deal with resistance to this belief.

> For I delivered to you as of first importance what I also received, that Christ died for our sins according to the Scriptures, and that He was buried, and that He was raised on the third day according to the Scriptures, and that He appeared to Cephas, then to the twelve. After that He appeared to more than five hundred brethren at one time, most of whom remain until now, but some have fallen asleep; then He appeared to James, then to all the apostles; and last of all, as it were to one untimely born, He appeared to me also (1 Corinthians 15:3-8).

Paul reminded the Corinthians of the gospel that he received, the good news that he preached to them. Christ died for our sins, he was buried, and he was raised on the third day. That was the gospel about Christ, that Paul and the apostles had preached to them. According to verse 11, that was the gospel they believed.

But something had happened between his visit and this letter. Somebody in Corinth had been teaching that although Christ was raised, there was no general resurrection of the dead.

> Now if Christ is preached, that He has been raised from the dead, how do some among you say that there is no resurrection of the dead? But if there is no resurrection of the dead, not even Christ has been raised; and if Christ has not been raised, then our preaching is vain, your faith also is vain . . . .
> For if the dead are not raised, not even Christ has been raised; and if Christ has not been raised, your faith is worthless. . . . Then those also who have fallen asleep in Christ have perished. If we have only hoped in Christ in this life, we are of all men most to be pitied (vv. 12-19).

Paul claims that when it comes to resurrection, you can't have one without the other. If there is no resurrection of the dead, then Christ has not been raised and our faith is vain, useless. And we are, of all people, most to be pitied.

"But now Christ has been raised from the dead, the first fruits of those who are asleep" (v. 20). A statement of fact! Christ has been raised from the dead. Christ's resurrection is not proven by the principle of the res-

urrection of the dead nor by the resurrection of
Lazarus or Dorcas or anyone else. It is the other way
around. Christ's resurrection is proven by eye witnesses. They saw him die, then they saw him alive!

The principle of the resurrection of the dead, both
of the wicked and the righteous, is proven by the fact
of the resurrection of Christ. It is Christ who is first in
this argument. We are not of all people most to be pitied, for Christ is the firstfruits of those who are dead,
those who are asleep. As by Adam death came, so also
by Christ came the resurrection of the dead. For as in
Adam all die, so also in Christ all shall be made alive
(vv. 21-22).

Here is a new image of God as the steward. God is
not only creator, and a good and prudent manager as
steward of creation, God is also a bit of a speculator.
God is an entrepreneur, willing to take risks with the
divine venture capital.

God took a risk and sent Jesus to die even while we
were still sinners and enemies. God then raised him
from the dead as a firstfruits offering so that we would
all be raised from the dead.

Here also is a new image of a firstfruits offering—
specifically, Christ, the firstfruits of the dead. Because
of Christ's resurrection there is a new connection between the dead and Christ. And the connection has to
do with Christ's being the firstfruits or the firstborn.

One of the best descriptions of that connection is in
Colossians 1:15-18.

> And He is the image of the invisible God, the first-born of
> all creation. For in Him all things were created, both in

the heavens and on the earth, visible and invisible,
whether thrones or dominions or rulers or authorities—
all things have been created through Him and for Him.
And He is before all things, and in Him all things hold together.
He is also head of the body, the church; and He is the beginning, the first-born from the dead; so that He Himself
might come to have first place in everything.

"He is before all things, and in Him all things hold
together." The word translated *hold together* means
"endure." All things endure. The connection is that
death has been changed because of Christ's resurrection and new position as the firstfruits of the dead. No
longer is death the end of everything; now death is en-
durable. Things do not fall apart in death now that Jesus has been raised from the dead. Now everything
holds together.

There is a future need to hold everything together
as well. Remember 1 Corinthians 15:22-25.

For as in Adam all die, so also in Christ all shall be made
alive. But each in his own order: Christ the first fruits,
after that those who are Christ's at His coming, then
comes the end, when He delivers up the kingdom to the
God and Father, when He has abolished all rule and all
authority and power. For He must reign until He has put
all His enemies under His feet.

All things need to hold together, to endure, because
God is not yet finished with creation, for we will all be
raised again. And Jesus raised from the dead is God's
firstfruits offering of what is still to come, the resurrection of the dead.

Jesus was raised from the dead, no matter what Ernst Troeltsch says. Eyewitnesses have told us so. Although the future resurrection of the dead is a matter of belief, lacking eyewitnesses, it is belief with a difference. Because Christ is the firstfruits of the dead, he is our evidence that we shall rise and endure past death.

As the firstfruits of creation and the dead, he is Lord and King of both life and death. He who is the firstfruits of the dead will reign over us through death, as he now reigns over us in life. "He lives, he lives, Christ Jesus lives today."

Questions to Ponder

1. We have been given the firstfruits offering of God's firstborn to show us the evidence of future plans for us. How might we make our offering a promise to God of our commitment to endure until God's plans are fulfilled?

2. How does the image of God the speculator, the entrepreneur who risks his own venture capital (Jesus), affect your image of what a steward does?

3. Are you a cautious or a risk-taking steward of what God has given you?

7

A Sign of the Promise, a Pledge of the Future

The rest of the villagers all said he was the kind of man who was impossible to please! This man would be unhappy no matter what you did. If he had been ill, his disease would be known as perpetual dissatisfaction, for indeed he complained about everything.

To be honest, as the villagers reluctantly admitted, his complaints were accurate. He did not have to make up things to complain about. But over the years the villagers tired of his bitter tongue and critical manner, especially when he was talking about their behavior.

And so one day, when they had had enough of him, the villagers formed a committee. With the village mayor as their spokesman, they went to the man to confront his negative and nasty attitude.

"You must stop it," they said. "You are making life miserable for everyone in the village."

"Life already is miserable," the man replied. "I'm not making it that way; you are. All I'm doing is pointing out how you are all making life miserable."

"We're doing the best we can," they told him. "We don't like living this way any more than you, but you have to be patient. Someday things will be better, in the days of the Promise."

"Someday? Someday?" snorted the man. "Someday isn't good enough. Why can't things get better now? Why not now, why not here?"

"What do you want from us?" asked the exasperated mayor.

"I want to live in a village where the people live in peace with their neighbors, instead of continually fighting and arguing like you do. I want to live in a village where the people respect the land and take care of it, instead of squeezing it dry every year to get the last ounce of profit from it.

"I want to live in a place where strangers are welcomed, instead of being run off by frightened people who care only for themselves. That's what I want. Is that too much to ask?"

The mayor shook his head. "Yes," he said, "that is way too much. You are a dreamer, if you think that is possible here and now. Maybe in the days of the Promise, maybe then. But not now.

"You can't be too careful, you know, especially about strangers. But even your neighbors will steal from you. And making your living from this poor land is hard enough. Yes, indeed, you do ask too much."

"Well I don't think it is too much," shouted the man at the crowd around his front door. "I don't think we have to wait until the Promise gets here to have these things. I think we could have them right here, right now, if you fools would stop acting like blithering idiots and try harder."

The mayor and the crowd retreated from this verbal onslaught and talked among themselves for a moment. Then the mayor turned to face the man. He said, "This is our decision. Since you are so ill-mannered, and since you will obviously not accept things the way they are, you are to be cast out from the village until old age has mellowed you."

With that the crowd surged forward. They grabbed the man, carried him to the fence that surrounded the village, and threw him over it. Others took his few belongings from his small house and threw them after him. Then, as the man slowly picked himself up from the dust, the crowd moved away into the alleys and streets of the village.

All except one person. An old woman, perhaps the oldest person in the village, hung back. And when she was sure no one was watching, she turned and faced the man in the dust.

"Listen," she whispered through the fence. "When I was a child I heard of a place where people live the way you want."

"Where is it?" asked the exiled man desperately. "How do you find that place?"

"If I knew I would have gone there myself," laughed the old woman. "But I think they said it was on the other side of the great woods to the north. You'll just have to find your own way."

The man picked himself up from the dust. He gathered what belongings he could carry and headed north, to the great woods.

Once he entered the woods he was immediately lost. There were a number of paths leading into the woods. Each path had as many as three forks. He despaired of finding the place of his dreams.

But one day, months after he had begun his journey, he came over a slight rise in the path. Ahead lay a city. Slowly he walked into the city. He asked the first person he met, "Is this the place of the Promise?"

"Promise? PROMISE?" shouted the man. "What do you mean—Promise?"

"I mean the place where people live in peace with their neighbors."

"Oh that," said the man. "The people you are looking for live over there on the other side of the city." And he pointed to a group of houses that were built facing each other.

The man ran over to those houses. Sure enough, these people actually loved their neighbors. "How do you do it?" he asked. "With all the thievery and suspicion and anger of the city around you, how can you live in peace?"

"Oh, we had heard about living this way since childhood," they replied. "But we were never able to actually do it—until one day a family moved here who had actually seen it done somewhere else. They did it here, and we copied them."

"Where is the place they came from," he asked, "where the people love each other and show great respect for the land and welcome strangers? The place of the Promise."

"Oh, that place," they said. "Yes, we know of a place like that, but it is far off. And the road to it is dangerous. You had better just settle here with us."

"No," the man replied, "I must find the place of the

Promise." And he turned and went on down the road and back into the dark woods.

Many weeks later, he came out of the woods to a village surrounded by farms. As he saw the green of the fields and the buildings of the farms, he thought surely this was the place where the people respected the land.

But then he began to notice washed-out gullies, steep slopes that were plowed, and sick-looking crops forced to grow on the slopes. In despair, he asked the first farmer he came to where the place of the Promise was.

"Promise?" came the gruff reply. "The only promise around here is the promise of working yourself to death at an early age. This land was worn out years ago by our fathers and grandfathers. It's all you can do to keep yourself in house and home, much less think about a promise."

Then the man noticed off in the distance an area much greener than the surrounding land. He asked, "What's that over there? Could that be the place of the Promise?"

"Nah! That's no promise. That's just a bunch of lucky amateurs. Why, they hardly farm at all, but I must admit they've sure been lucky. It doesn't seem to rain anymore on their side of the valley—but it must, since their crops are healthier than anything on this side.

"They're not of much account, though. They live in little houses. They own little. Who wants to be poor like them? That's not much of a promise!"

"Thank you," said the man. "That's the place I'm

looking for." And he headed off to the green farmland.

When he got there, he asked the first person he saw how they had learned to live with respect for the land.

The woman told him, "At first we were like everyone else. We squeezed every drop of profit we could out of our land. The land suffered, but we didn't know any other way.

"And then, on a visit to my relatives in another valley, we saw a man farming this way. We stayed with him for a season and learned from him."

"Then that must be the place of the Promise," the man said.

"Oh, no," said the woman. "If you want the place of the Promise, you must continue on over that far mountain range and beyond."

And so the man went on his way once more. After many more months of searching, he came over a hill. He saw in the distance, in the fading daylight, a village nestled in the valley below.

It was late when he reached the village, well past midnight. At first the man thought the moonlight was playing tricks with his eyes. For, oddly enough, this village looked a lot like his own.

In fact, at the end of a vaguely familiar street, was a house that looked like his old one. Carefully, he pushed the unlocked door open and went in. Sure enough. It was his home.

Then he remembered the order expelling him from the village until he was mellowed by old age. He turned to flee. But he was too tired to continue. *I'll just rest here for a few hours*, he thought. *Then I'll be on my way in the dark of the early morning.*

Well, he slept longer than he had planned. And when he woke it was light and too late to escape without being seen.

What was worse, his neighbors had noticed that someone had broken into his home during the night. They had called the mayor and the constable to come investigate; at this very moment they were approaching the door. He was trapped!

He decided to make the best of it. What else could he do? When they came through the open front door, he met them with a smile and an outstretched hand. "Hello, my old friends," he said. "Welcome to my home."

"Who are you?" they demanded. "What's this about 'old friends,' and why have you broken into another man's house?"

"But I am that other man," said the man softly.

"Impossible," said the constable. "I admit you look a little bit like him. But he was an old grouch who never had a kind word for any of us."

"It *is* me," insisted the man, who by now was finding the whole thing funny and was starting to grin.

"Nonsense!" said the mayor. "But you look like a friendly enough fellow. Tell you what, why don't you stay here until that old grouch comes back? He's off looking for perfect people who live in the perfect village. He'll be gone a long, long time, looking for such a place as that."

"I know what you mean," said the man. "I know what you mean. But as long as you're here," he continued, "why don't you sit down? I'll make some tea, then I'll tell you about how people live where I come from."

Questions to Ponder

1. What land of Promise are you looking for?

2. In what ways have you traveled far, only to find that what you want was already at home, waiting to be found?

3. Read the Beatitudes at the beginning of the Sermon on the Mount as if they were Jesus' description of the place of Promise. How could the church live out in small ways, here and now, these aspects of the Promise?

8

God's Engagement Ring for Us

In December of 1964 when I proposed marriage to my wife, I gave her a small diamond ring as a sign of our engagement. I don't remember my exact thoughts at the time, but, looking back, I am surprised at myself. I am a very practical person. And a bit thrifty. I like doing without, finding ways to do things without spending money.

Of all the things people buy for each other, a diamond engagement ring is surely the most expensive and least practical. Diamond rings don't actually do anything for the engagement or the marriage. Engagement is a mutual commitment, not a ring with a stone in the middle. And anyway, a wedding band will soon replace the ring. About the only thing you can do with an engagement ring is show it to your friends. They promptly ignore it and begin asking questions about the wedding.

Yet the diamond business flourishes. Millions of diamond engagement rings are sold each year. I suspect there is a good reason. At the beginning of the relationship, a couple is just beginning to trust each other's commitments. The commitment to marry is simultaneously one of the earliest and one of the most significant commitments of the entire relationship. The engagement ring is a sign of that commitment. We spend great sums of money on these impractical items to assure each other of our intentions.

The apostle Paul knows something about commitments for the future.

> We know that the whole creation groans and suffers the pains of childbirth together until now. And not only this, but also we ourselves, having the first fruits of the Spirit, even we ourselves groan within ourselves, waiting eagerly for our adoption as sons, the redemption of our body (Romans 8:22-23).

We, who have the firstfruits of the Spirit, now wait eagerly for the future, even groaning as we do so. The presence of the Spirit's firstfruits within us affects how we wait for what Paul calls our adoption and our redemption.

Waiting for the redemption, the resurrection we discussed in chapter seven, is hard enough. But without the Holy Spirit within us, it would be much more difficult to faithfully wait. Paul says that he considers the present sufferings to be nothing compared with the glory to come; the single focus of the entire creation is toward that moment.

A part of that focus is something that you can see around you right now. I suspect that if you asked, most people would admit wondering whether all this stuff about judgment, the book of life, and the lake of fire is really going to happen. There is no more serious question about the future than that, for if God is really here and that is really true, a lot of people are going to be in big trouble.

We who are Christians are not immune to that sort of anxiety, or groaning as Paul calls it. You don't have to look far in a Christian bookstore to find a long list of books about whether there is an end and what will happen then.

In Romans 8, Paul is telling us that, even though we have the firstfruits of the Holy Spirit, we also groan and wait eagerly. But I get the idea that having the firstfruits of the Spirit is supposed to make a difference in how we wait.

In Ephesians 1:13-14 Paul says,

> In Him, you also, after listening to the message of truth, the gospel of your salvation—having also believed, you were sealed in Him with the Holy Spirit of promise, who is given as a pledge of our inheritance, with a view to the redemption of God's own possession, to the praise of His glory.

The Holy Spirit of promise seals us in God. The Holy Spirit is given to us as a pledge that God will redeem God's possession—namely, us.

The word *pledge* here means the first payment on something, like a down payment. It means not having the whole thing but having at least a foretaste of the thing. A small part is given as a promise and a pledge of the whole that is to come.

The Holy Spirit within us is one down payment of

the redemption. Perhaps a good symbol to put near that word would be a giant diamond engagement ring. The engagement ring is not the same as a marriage, but it is a pledge toward the marriage.

In 2 Corinthians 1:21-22, Paul refers again to a pledge: "Now He who establishes us with you in Christ and anointed us is God, who also sealed us and gave us the Spirit in our hearts as a pledge." This is another reference to the Spirit as a pledge, as a foretaste of what is to come.

God has brought us forth by the word of truth, to be the firstfruits among God's creatures. We can be those firstfruits because God's Spirit is given to us as part of the process of sealing us in Christ.

In these firstfruits acts of God, it is God who is the good steward. God as Creator is practicing godly stewardship over creation. God as steward gives us a firstfruits offering of the Holy Spirit as an engagement ring, promising the coming of the kingdom, and our eternal life with God.

Questions to Ponder

1. God has given us an offering of the Holy Spirit as a pledge of his final redemption of us. What offering might we make in return as an "engagement ring" or pledge of our commitment to God?

2. How could our weekly firstfruits offering be made a pledge to God, proclaiming that we are committed to God to the end?

3. What about our time? Could an offering of a term of voluntary service somewhere in our "marriage" with God serve as a sign of our commitment?

9

The Rabbi's Gift

There was once a famous monastery which had fallen on hard times. Formerly, its many buildings were filled with young monks, and its big church resounded with the singing of the chant. It was known far and wide as a place of godly people. Many people came to it for spiritual guidance and nourishment.

Now it was almost deserted. People no longer came to be nourished by prayer. No one came to be strengthened by retreat. A handful of old monks shuffled through the cloisters and praised their God, but they did so with heavy hearts. The abbot spent many hours in prayer, asking God to send a renewal to these faithful monks.

On the edge of the monastery woods, an old Jewish rabbi had built a little hut. He would come there from time to time to fast and pray.

No one ever spoke with him. But whenever he appeared, the word would be passed from monk to monk, "The rabbi walks in the woods." As long as he was there, the monks would feel sustained by his prayerful presence.

One day, the abbot decided to visit the rabbi and open his heart to him. After morning eucharist, he set out through the woods. As he approached the hut, the abbot saw the rabbi standing in the doorway, his arms outstretched in welcome. It was as though he knew that the abbot would come and had been waiting there for him.

The two embraced like long-lost brothers. Then they stepped back. They just stood there, smiling at each other with smiles their faces could hardly contain.

After a while, the rabbi motioned the abbot to enter. In the middle of the one room was a wooden table with the Scriptures open on it. They sat there for a moment in the presence of the Book.

Then, to the astonishment of the abbot, the rabbi began to cry. The abbot could no longer contain himself and began to cry, too. For the first time in his life, he cried his heart out in the presence of another man. The two men sat there like lost children, filling the hut with their sobs and wetting the wooden table with their tears.

After the tears had ceased to flow and all was quiet again, the rabbi lifted his head. "You and your brothers are serving God with heavy hearts," he said. "You have come to ask a teaching of me. I will give you a teaching, but you must not repeat it to anyone. For if you do, on that day surely you will die."

The rabbi looked straight at the abbot, and then he said in a quiet hushed voice, "The Messiah is among you."

For a while, all was silent. Then the rabbi said, "Now you must go."

The abbot left without a word and without looking back.

The next morning, the abbot called his monks together in the chapel room. He told them he had received a teaching from the rabbi who walks in the woods. He was forbidden to repeat the teaching. But he was sure that this teaching was from God and would change their situation.

Change things it certainly did. Each time the abbot saw one of the monks he thought, *Is Brother John the Messiah? Or Father Matthew? Or Brother Thomas? Or am I the Messiah? What does this mean, the Messiah is among you?*

At first the change was only noticeable in the abbot. The other monks noticed that he began to treat them all with a special reverence. It was as if he had seen something special in each of them. They each felt special when he talked or worked with them.

After a while, the monks themselves began to change. There was a gentle, wholehearted, human quality about them now that was hard to describe but easy to notice. They lived with one another as men who had found something. But they prayed the Scriptures together as men who were always looking for something.

Occasional visitors found themselves deeply moved by the life of these monks. Before long, people were coming from far and wide to be nourished by the prayer life of the monks. Young men were asking, once again, to become part of this holy community.

In those days, the rabbi no longer walked in the woods. In fact, after the abbot's visit, no one had seen the rabbi again. Then the abbot grew old and fell ill.

Fearful that the teaching that had brought about such spiritual renewal to the monastery would be lost forever, the monks gathered around his bed. They pled with him to reveal the secret of their renewed faith.

Knowing this was the day he was to die, the abbot called them near to his bed. In the whisper of a man about to meet God, he said for the first time those supremely powerful words, the gift from the rabbi who walked in the woods. "The Messiah is among you."

Questions to Ponder

1. Has anyone ever treated you differently this way?

2. How might the Rabbi's gift change the spiritual life of your church?

3. People who start to practice firstfruits giving, taking their offering from the first of what they earn, often report that the rest of their earnings seem to have changed as a result.

How might this work? Does God somehow honor our firstfruits offering by taking charge of the rest of what God has given us as well?

10

The Firstfruits Offering and Everything Else

A good way to define something unfamiliar is to describe it in terms of the difference between it and something else which is familiar. At this point in our exploration of the concept of firstfruits offering, we will do exactly that. We will look at the relationship between the firstfruits and everything else. This is a relationship of difference, specifically the difference between the holy and the profane.

The idea of something being holy is present in God's work from the beginning. "Then God blessed the seventh day and sanctified it [made it holy], because in it He rested from all His work which God had created and made" (Genesis 2:3).

Here is the definition of holiness. There is something different about that seventh day, something that sets it apart from the other six days. On that day God rested instead of worked. What sets apart the holy from the common is that it is set apart, it is different.

"Holy," or "sanctified" is the meaning of the word

qadosh. The related verb used here literally means to separate, to set apart from the rest. Something that is holy is set apart from the rest.

The most holy thing that exists is God, and God is certainly set apart from everything else. A constant theme in the Law is that the creator is different than the creation.

Anything that God calls holy is set apart. The Sabbath is holy, because it is set apart from the other days of the week. We do different things on the Sabbath, simply because it is a set-apart day. In Jeremiah 17:21-22, we get a good definition of what makes the Sabbath holy.

> Thus says the Lord, "Take heed for yourselves, and do not carry any load on the sabbath day or bring anything in through the gates of Jerusalem. And you shall not bring a load out of your houses on the sabbath day nor do any work, but keep the sabbath day holy, as I commanded your forefathers."

The Sabbath is not holy simply because it is the Sabbath. It is holy because, and only because, we treat it differently than any other day of the week.

The sanctuary of the church building can be a holy place, not because the bricks and wood and carpet were delivered directly from heaven instead of a factory, but because it is a set-apart place. It is different from other places.

We choose not to do some things in our places of worship because we have made them holy places. We have set them apart from all other places and all other activities. It is our choice that makes them holy.

Other things are holy as well, not because they were manufactured holy or born holy, but because they were made holy by being set apart. In Exodus 13:1-2 we hear the Lord's instruction to Moses about the first-born. "Then the Lord spoke to Moses, saying, 'Sanctify [make holy, set apart] to Me every first-born, the first offspring of every womb among the sons of Israel, both of man and beast; it belongs to Me.'"

In Numbers 18:17 we find that having been set apart, the firstborn are now holy. "'But the first-born of an ox or . . . a sheep or . . . a goat, you shall not redeem; they are holy [set apart].'"

That is our first lesson for this chapter: the firstfruits are not holy simply because of what they are. They are holy because they have been set apart.

The firstfruits offerings that the Levites received from the people of Israel were holy not because they were great offerings. They were holy because they were set apart from the other things people owned and used.

People are holy as well. And for the same reason. Listen to Leviticus 20:24-26.

Hence I have said to you, "You are to possess their land, and I Myself will give it to you to possess it, a land flowing with milk and honey." I am the Lord your God, who has separated you from the peoples. You are therefore to make a distinction between a clean animal and the unclean, and between the unclean bird and the clean; and you shall not make yourselves detestable by animal or by bird or by anything that creeps on the ground, which I have separated for you as unclean. Thus you are to be

holy to Me, for I the Lord am holy; and I have set you
apart from the peoples to be Mine.

The people of God were set apart and therefore
holy. They were separated from other peoples. There
was a distinction between them and others, as well as a
distinction between the clean and unclean things they
might eat. Maintaining that distinction is the subject of
at least half of the book of Leviticus.

We are a holy people as well. As we discovered earlier, in 1 Peter 2:5 we who have received mercy because of the grace of Christ are being built up as a spiritual house for a holy priesthood. We are a set-apart
priesthood.

In verse 9, we are called a holy nation, a people set
apart from all others. We are set apart not in a national
identity such as American or Canadian, but a nation
called Christians. We are set apart by our obedience to
the call of Christ.

What makes us holy is being separated from the
rest. As the Sabbath is holy because it is treated like no
other day, so we are holy when set aside and separated. God's holy work is done. We have been set apart
and separated from slavery to sin by the shed blood of
Christ.

But even though we have been set apart, some of us
want to go back to Egypt and our slavery. That was the
experience during the Exodus from Egypt. It was the
experience of Israel throughout her history.

Eventually the Lord sent the nation into exile because of their sin of not being a set-apart or holy people. Ezekiel receives a vision of how the Lord is going

to restore Israel. Listen to how things have changed from the holiness of the Levites:

> But the Levites who went far from Me, when Israel went astray, who went astray from Me after their idols, shall bear the punishment for their iniquity. . . . And they shall not come near to Me to serve as a priest to Me, nor come near to any of My holy things, to the things that are most holy; but they shall bear their shame and their abominations which they have committed (Ezekiel 44:10, 13).

The Lord goes on to say that the sons of Zadok, the only ones who have stayed holy by remaining separated from the idols, will teach the people the difference between the holy and the profane.

Becoming firstfruits, set-apart people, is rooted in God's work. But staying firstfruits, separated people, is a matter of faithfulness. Just as the Israelites wanted to go back to Egypt when the going got rough, so we want to stop being separated. That is the challenge. How do we remain set apart? We usually think of firstfruits as giving to God the first of what God gives to us. When we do that we set apart, separate, that part from the rest. We take from the first of what we get, and we make it holy by separating it from ourselves.

We set money apart by putting it into the offering. It becomes holy because it is set apart from the rest of our money. That is a practical thing. It is something all of us can do, no matter how big the pile of fruit is.

But income is just one thing that is a firstfruits in our lives. Remember, *we* are firstfruits. We are that holy, set-apart nation.

What about our time? If we, only because of our salvation through Christ, are holy then should not our time be holy as well? How do we devote our time so that it is holy, set apart? Is there a difference between how we spend the first of our time and how the society around us spends the first of its time?

As we have already discovered from the Scriptures, things that are not really the first can be declared firstfruits and set apart in holiness. A good way to make time holy is "vacations with a purpose." Instead of taking a vacation simply to fill the time, these vacations are short-term voluntary service opportunities.

There is an added benefit to this idea of the first being holy. It is hinted at in Romans 11:16. "And if the first piece of dough [meaning the Jews] be holy, then the lump [or the Gentiles] is also; and if the root be holy, then the branches are too."

If the first piece is holy, then so is the rest. What would happen if we took that to be a promise of what is possible, rather than simply a description of history? What if we took this verse as a suggestion or an instruction on how to turn the common or the profane into the holy? What if we understood this verse to say that if the first of something is made holy by being set apart, then the rest of it is made holy as well?

We do not have to stretch the verse to do just that.

For if by the transgression of the one, death reigned through the one, much more those who receive the abundance of grace and of the gift of righteousness will reign in life through the One, Jesus Christ. So then as through one transgression there resulted condemnation to all men, even so through one act of righteousness there resulted justification of life to all men. For as through the

one man's disobedience the many were made sinners,
even so through the obedience of the One the many will
be made righteous (Romans 5:17-19).

From one profane act of one man, Adam, sin entered the world, and through sin, death. But the abundance of grace and of the gift of righteousness was received through Jesus Christ, the firstfruits of God. One
wayward lamb misled the whole flock. But one holy
Lamb has redeemed the whole flock.

If the first is made holy, the rest can be made holy as
well. And if we are holy, then we will make a difference. That will be the measure of our holiness and the
holiness of our firstfruits offerings—not that we or
they are so different, but that those differences have
made a difference.

Just as the holiness of Christ has changed us, so our
holiness should change others. We and our firstfruits
offerings are to be the infecting agents of God. We are
to infect others with the kingdom of God, until there is
a worldwide epidemic of holiness.

Questions to Ponder

1. What things in our lives do we consider holy?
Our marriages, our children, our cars? How do we set
them apart in holiness?

2. Have you ever been affected by something or
someone that you would consider holy, or separated?

3. Through what behaviors might we affect our
neighbors in a holy way?

11

The Barefoot People

Once there was a man who had business in a far country that he had never visited. As he arrived at the country's airport and stepped out of the plane, he noticed it was quite cold; there was snow on the ground. This was not so unusual, since it was winter.

But then he noticed something that *was* unusual. The ground crew around the plane were all barefoot! As cold as it was and as uncomfortable as it must have been, no one working out there had shoes on.

As he walked down the concourse toward the baggage area, he noticed other airport employees without shoes. Just to be sure, he glanced down at his own feet. He was relieved to see he still wore shoes. The other passengers also wore shoes. But the gate attendants, ticket agents, and baggage handlers were barefoot.

Now this is an odd practice, the man thought, as he claimed his baggage and headed for the car rental agency. But he resisted the temptation to stop one of the barefoot people and ask why they wore no shoes.

He resisted, that is, until he noticed that the man who walked him out to his rental car, through the snow and ice, also wore no shoes. Unable to restrain himself, he asked the man how this unusual practice had begun.

"What practice?" asked the barefoot man.

"Why," said the business man, pointing to those bare feet, "why don't people at this airport wear shoes?"

"Ahhh," the barefoot man said. "Yes, well, that's just it. Why don't we, indeed?"

"Well," the traveler asked, "what is it? Don't you believe in shoes?"

"Believe in shoes! I should say that we believe in shoes! That is the first article of our national constitution—shoes. They are indispensable to the well-being of our citizens. Such frostbite, cuts, sores, and suffering as shoes prevent—they are indeed wonderful things!"

"Well, then, why don't you wear them?"

"Ahhh," said the man again, "That is just it. Why don't we, indeed?"

Considerably confused, the traveler got in the car. He left the man standing barefoot in a shallow puddle of icy slush and drove into the city. When he found his hotel, he checked in. Then he went down to the coffee shop and deliberately sat next to an amiable looking but barefoot gentleman. Friendly enough, the barefoot gentleman suggested that, after they had eaten, he would show the traveler around the city.

The first thing that they noticed on emerging from the hotel was a huge brick building. It was an impressive structure indeed. The man pointed to it and said with considerable pride, "You see that? It is one of our most outstanding shoe factories!"

"A what?" the traveler asked in amazement. "You mean you make shoes in there?"

"Well, not exactly make them," said the man. "Actually we talk about making shoes in there, and believe me, when it comes to shoes, in there we have one of the most brilliant fellows you have ever heard. He talks most thrillingly and convincingly every week on this great subject of shoes.

"Just yesterday he moved his listeners profoundly with his exposition on the necessity of shoe wearing. Many broke down and wept. And many made enthusiastic first-time commitments concerning the importance of wearing shoes."

"But why don't they wear them?" the traveler asked in astonishment.

"Ahhh, yes," he said. "That is just it. Why, indeed, don't we?"

Turning down a side street, they saw through a cellar window a man actually making what looked like shoes. Excusing himself from his new friend, the traveler burst into the cobbler's shop. He asked the shoemaker why his shop was not overrun with customers.

"Well," the shoemaker said, "nobody actually wants my shoes. They just talk about them."

"Give me what pairs you have ready," the traveler said eagerly. He paid twice the modest amount the cobbler asked.

Hurriedly the traveler returned to his friend and offered the shoes to him. "Here, my friend, one of these pairs will surely fit you. Take them, put them on. They will save you untold suffering."

"Ahhh, thank you," the friend said, looking around with some embarrassment. "But you don't understand. It just isn't being done. Not even the most enthusiastic actually wear shoes. Nobody seems to know why. Maybe it is because we don't know how, maybe they are too expensive, maybe people actually like being barefoot.

"But one thing is certain. It just isn't being done. That is a good question, Why don't we? Why don't we?"

Questions to Ponder

1. Why don't we wear "shoes"? How are we Christians like the barefoot people who preach but don't live the value of shoes?

2. What does it take to make a good idea part of our behavior?

3. What experiences have you had that have changed, not only your mind, but also your way of living? What was it about those experiences that made the crucial difference, that moved you from preaching about shoes to wearing shoes?

12

Defending Against Robbery on the High Seas

One of the most popular of the Broadway shows turned into a movie was *The Music Man*. Professor Harold Hill was a flimflam man trying to sell musical instruments and band uniforms to children who did not know how to play or march. The scam was that he did not know how to play the instruments himself, much less teach them.

But his big selling point to the parents was that having their children in the band would keep them out of trouble, specifically, out of the town pool hall.

In one of the musical numbers early in the film, Professor Hill sings about trouble: "We got trouble, big, big, big trouble, right here in River City. It begins with *t* and that rhymes with *p* and that stands for pool. Yessir, trouble, we sure got trouble."

As far as the apostle James is concerned, the first-century church "got trouble" also. And this trouble also begins with a *t*, and that rhymes with three, and that stands for trials, and testing and temptation.

"Yessir, we got trouble," James says, "we got trials and testings and temptations."

James is a practical man, and the book of James is a practical book. James could be seen as wanting to bring the readers of the apostle Paul back down to earth. Paul expected Jesus to return any day, but James wrote later than Paul, probably after Paul's death at Rome. Jesus had not come yet.

What was worse, by this time there were some real problems arising in the lives of believers. They were not problems of correct doctrine, but problems of correct behavior. The excitement of conversion and Pentecost had faded into the past. The old nature had reared its ugly head.

James has a message for those who "got trouble." As James sees it, trouble can yield two possible outcomes. There are two ways we can walk when trouble comes. First James show the way we should go.

> Consider it all joy, my brethren, when you encounter various trials, knowing that the testing of your faith produces endurance. And let endurance have its perfect results, that you may be perfect and complete, lacking in nothing. But if any of you lacks wisdom, let him ask of God, who gives to all men generously and without reproach, and it will be given to him (James 1:2-5).

A fruit of successfully going through trials is endurance, and having endurance makes us whole and complete. But you don't get endurance without going through trials. So consider it joy when you encounter trials. That is the way to get endurance, which makes a whole and complete believer.

Now that is an interesting thought—that the way to become complete is to have trouble. How often do we find ourselves praying for a trouble-free life, happy and blissful, without trials and tribulations? But James says that without trials you cannot become whole and complete as a Christian. You need trouble to develop.

One of my wife's hobbies is raising quail to release into the wild. When Linda's quail eggs started to hatch, we noticed that quail hatch by pecking out a round door in the big end of the egg. That looked like a lot of work. We wanted to help a few of the weaker ones by opening the egg for them.

But quail experts advise against that. The struggle to get out of the egg is part of the bird's development. It needs to struggle to become a complete bird. Sure enough, the few birds we did help did not develop into strong and mature quail. That is what James is saying about trials. We need them to become strong and mature Christians.

Consider making a note in your Bible to remember what James is trying to say. First, above the word *trials* (or *temptations* in some versions) in James 1:2, put a little skull-and-crossbones symbol. That was the symbol all the famous or infamous pirates had on their flags. The reason I want you to put it there is that James' original word is *pirasmoi*, from which we get the word *piracy*.

The definition of *piracy* is an act of robbery on the high seas. A temptation or trial is like a robbery on the high seas. You are merrily sailing along, when suddenly your happy life is run down and attacked by this pirate ship called trouble. But, James says, when you encounter the pirate ship of trouble, know that the testing of your faith produces endurance.

Here is the second note you might want to put in your Bible. Above the words "the testing [or trying] of your faith" in verse 3, put a thumbs-up sign. A fist with the thumb sticking up is a sign of approval.

That is what that phrase means. "The testing of your faith" actually means "the part of your faith that is approved." If that doesn't make immediate sense to you, think of an inspector at the end of an assembly line in a toaster factory. The inspector plugs in the finished toasters and the coils get red hot. If the thing doesn't blow a fuse or catch on fire during its testing, it is approved. The inspector puts a little thumbs-up sticker on the toaster to indicate that it will endure being used.

After a short diversion into the troubles that come from being either poor or rich, James returns in verse 12 to this issue of piracy. "Blessed is a man who perseveres under trial; for once he has been approved, he will receive the crown of life, which the Lord has promised to those who love Him."

That is the good news. Trials are supposed to produce endurance by testing our faith. Those who persevere will receive God's seal of approval.

Now comes the bad news. Even in the church, it doesn't always work out that way.

> Let no one say when he is tempted, "I am being tempted by God"; for God cannot be tempted by evil, and He Himself does not tempt any one. But each one is tempted when he is carried away and enticed by his own lust. Then when lust has conceived, it give birth to sin; and

when sin is accomplished [or fully formed, or mature], it
brings forth death (James 1:13-15).

Now I don't know what you think when you hear
the word *lust*. I suppose most people think of sexual
emotions. But lust simply means having a passion
about anything. Lust is desire with a fire under it. It is
covetousness with a vengeance. It is want with force.
Lust is not simply interest in something, or desire for
something. Lust is "I want it bad, and I want it now!"

James tells us that when we are carried away by passion about something, we are subject to piracy, to
temptation. Notice that it is not the existence of a passionate desire that tempts us. Being carried away and
enticed by passion is the problem. Lust is not the problem. But it is where the problem comes from.

James is telling us that temptation comes when we
give in to lust. Then, when lust has conceived, when it
begins to grow and develop because it was given in to,
it gives birth to sin. And when that sin is accomplished,
fully formed, it brings death. James is pretty clear that
at least some of our trouble comes from yielding to
and being carried away by our own passionate desires.

We are not to be deceived by saying that our trouble
is coming from God. Have you heard yourself or
someone else say in the middle of trouble, "I am being
tested by God"? But James would say, "I am indeed being tested, but by my own passion, not by God."

There you have it, two ways to deal with piracy in
our lives. We can give in and be carried away by our
passions. This will lead to sin, which will lead to death.
Or we can persevere and endure, which will lead to

wholeness and completeness, to life.

James shows that our struggle between yielding to or overcoming lust matters, not only to us, but to the world, which needs us to model godly lives.

> Do not be deceived, my beloved brethren. Every good thing bestowed and every perfect gift is from above, coming down from the Father of lights, with whom there is no variation, or shifting shadow. In the exercise of His will He brought us forth by the word of truth, so that we might be, as it were, the firstfruits among His creatures (James 1:16-18).

God has brought us forth, as believers, to be firstfruits of the creation. Remember, the firstfruits offering is anything set apart which has an effect on the rest. That is what we are to be to the rest of God's creatures. In some sense, we are the good and perfect gift to creation, an offering of a good and beneficent God.

God chose to call us out of the world, to be separated unto God, to be a model of perseverance and endurance in the face of trials and temptations and piracy on the high seas. We as God's firstfruits offering are to be a model to the rest of the creation.

Questions to Ponder

1. If we are to be models to the rest of God's creatures, what are we modeling? How would you describe the image you are trying to model?

2. If our lives are to be visible examples of firstfruits living, how can they become one with our theology?

13

Living as Signs of the Coming Kingdom

Sometimes we look in all the wrong places for all the right things. Twentieth-century theology is a lot like that. We know, as Paul has told us, that the kingdom of God is not eating and drinking. It is righteousness and peace and joy in the Holy Spirit.

But many in the church today have somehow assumed that righteousness and peace and joy will only come when Jesus comes again. Too many Christians have given up on the commandments of Christ in the here and now. They are just waiting around for that new order to come when we will have his power and his authority to live his way.

That is like people living in a bus stop in the middle of a slum. They wait for the celestial bus to come and rescue them. In the meantime, they make the bus stop a fortress, protecting themselves from the evil outside. Occasionally, in the name of "mission," they snatch someone from the slum and take him into the bus stop to wait with them.

But Jesus says that the kingdom of God does not come full grown. It comes instead like a tiny mustard seed which grows and becomes a tree. It comes in the mean streets surrounding that bus stop, which those waiting might see if they only paid attention to the little signs of hope instead of pining for the bus.

No, the kingdom of God does not happen all at once. Jesus says it is like leaven—you put a little bit in the dough and, after a while, when it has grown and multiplied, the whole pile of dough is leavened. A little makes a big difference (Luke 13:18-21).

We know the difference the gospel of Christ is supposed to make in us. But sometimes we end up looking for that difference in the wrong places. What about the difference it is supposed to make outside of us?

In addition to changing our eternal destination, can the gospel of Christ make a difference in how we deal with conflict? Can it change how we relate to the government? To whom we pledge allegiance? Where we find our entertainment? With whom we associate?

As Christians, we want all areas of our lives to be affected by our new birth experience, by our regeneration, by our faith in Christ and his gospel. The sixteenth-century Anabaptists came to a fundamental but radical understanding. Seeking to carry Luther's and Zwingli's reformation to its logical fullness, they concluded that the inner new birth experience is seen in an outer change of living.

God calls us to live in peace, but not in a fortified bus stop. God calls us to be out in the neighborhood, redeeming and transforming the brokenness around us by being a model of what is to come.

That is the teaching of Jesus Christ—that the kingdom of God will not be over there or out there. It is already in our midst. That is the core of Anabaptist theology. If any group of believers understood the kingdom of God, it was those early Anabaptists who refused to limit faith in Christ to personal salvation and a change in eternal destination.

For them, as it must be for us, the kingdom of God was realized in the small communities which sprang up everywhere. These small circles of Christian love and sharing and nonresistance pointed the way to the kingdom to come.

In addition, our regenerated lives are not to be isolated examples of transformation, stuck away in a corner of the world's bus stops. We are not made new creatures in Christ simply so that we will become more likable or more effective or more holy for our own benefit.

We are not reborn simply as a symbol of what salvation is all about. We are instead transformed by the new birth into the *firstfruits offering of God*. We, like Christ, are the firstfruits of the resurrection, signs of the coming kingdom.

Suppose you hear a ship's foghorn. The foghorn is not itself the ship, but it is a part of the ship. And it tells you that, although you can't see it through the fog, a ship is indeed coming.

Living as a *firstfruits offering* is being a foghorn in the gloom of the present darkness. It is a sign that something is coming. Even though we can't see it through the fog of a troubled world, God's ship is coming, and our lives as firstfruits are its foghorn.

Living as a *firstfruits offering* is a little piece of that new order to come. It is not the whole kingdom of God already here. But it is a piece of the whole that will come on the day Jesus returns. Living as a firstfruits offering is living in small ways the new order that will be brought by the coming of Christ.

For example, living as a firstfruits offering is living at peace with one another now, not waiting for Jesus to come in the air to make it easy to live in peace. It means living in peace, not because we deserve peace or always want peace, but because it is a sign of what we can expect in the full kingdom to come.

Living as a firstfruits offering is living in harmony with God's created universe. Not because it pays or because it is popular to care for the earth, but because that is the way it is going to be in the coming new order.

Living as a firstfruits offering is being a welcomer of the stranger and a lover of the enemy now. Not because it is effective in reducing crime or war, but as a foretaste of the welcome and love strangers and enemies will receive in the kingdom of God.

Our model of stewardship is not the servant who buried his talent in the ground, trying to preserve it. It is not even following Christ's suggestion that it would have been better to have put it in the bank where it could draw interest. Living as a firstfruit offering is living in an entrepreneurial relationship with life, including our use of the material things that come our way.

From our study of firstfruits, it is clear that, at least in God's eyes, some kinds of money are different than other kinds. The first of our income, for example, is special because it belongs to God. The first kind of money is firstfruits money.

But what about the rest of our money? In 2 Corinthians 9:8, while encouraging the Corinthians to be generous in the special gift they are preparing for the Macedonians, the apostle Paul defines for us the other two kinds of money. "And God is able to make all grace abound to you, that always having all sufficiency in everything, you may have an abundance for every good deed." The second kind of money is that which is for "having all sufficiency in everything." This is money for our needs. God wants us to have our needs met.

But God wants us to have more than our needs require. This third kind of money is the "abundance for every good deed." Since Paul is speaking in the context of raising a gift to be sent to the Macedonians, we can be sure that the "abundance" is not given to us for our luxuries or for an expansion of our "needs." It is given for every good deed, deeds that fill the needs of others.

The problem for many of us is that, although we may give a firstfruits offering, we never seem to have the abundance for the good works God sends our way. That is because most of us do not really know where our needs end. We will not know until we begin to keep track of where we are spending the money God makes available to us. This is why record keeping taught in books on Christian money management is so important to Christian stewardship.

The best model I am aware of for managing the abundance is the "giving account" or "God's account" idea. Many people transfer what is left over each month from their household account into a separate account. That separate account is then a collection of God's money. It is money given to them by God specifically for giving to good deeds.

My personal experience is that just setting up a God's account is a witness to the people at the bank. Giving away someone else's money also added a great deal of joy to our giving. Now we don't have to worry whether we can afford to give to a particular need. If the money is in God's account, then that is exactly what it is for.

Our model in spending God's money is the risk-taking, entrepreneurial God. This God invests the ultimate venture capital, God's only Son, in the risky business of saving us.

Even with the foreknowledge that the market was shaky, even with the awareness that the product would be scorned by many, God the steward risked the Son on our behalf, for our profit. Even while we were yet sinners and enemies, Christ died for us.

Living as God's firstfruits offering means living as entrepreneurs of the gospel. It means putting our money and our time to use as signs of the kingdom of God. It is offering to God from the first of what we receive, before calculating the risk or counting the cost, before deciding if we can afford to be God's kind of steward.

As believers in Christ, we are called to be signs of the kingdom of God. We model what the kingdom, in its fullness, will be like. We are heralds of what is to come.

Things to Ponder

1. How do you keep track of God's money? How do you determine where your needs end? What do you think of setting up a separate account to hold and spend for God any money left over after needs are met?

2. What difference might it make to experience ourselves as spending God's money instead of our own?

3. In what ways is your life a foghorn? In what ways could it be?

Guide for Discussion Leaders and Groups

Welcome to an important experience in your life! All of us are deeply involved in issues addressed in this book. *Firstfruits* is one window through which to view much of the Biblical message; it invites us to give "our best to God." One way to think of your task as a leader is to expect new understandings worth sharing. Another way is to ask, "How can I make the invitation clear to each member so they give their very best?"

You will have succeeded when *Firstfruits Living: Giving God Our Best* helps each participant develop deeper commitment to living *out* God's firstfruits gifts to us and to living *out* the intentions of this God for humankind. These pages are written to help that happen. What should you do?

1. Know and use these materials. You have two kinds of material—the stories and the Bible studies. Stories invite all kinds of people to become involved. When we used the materials at Deep Run Mennonite Church

East, we gave a copy of the stories to each household and asked everyone to read the story in preparation for that day's study. Then in the worship service we had the stories read aloud. The congregation, including the children, was attentive while the stories were read. One member said he doesn't read that much, but the first Sunday afternoon he had the stories, he read them all.

Expect that people will find all kinds of things in the stories. When you invite them to share, accept what they have found. Learn from their findings. Be especially attentive to feelings released by the stories. We often find it hard to express our feelings; stories can help us.

The second resource is inductive Bible studies. Lynn gets hold of a text about firstfruits and begins to "shake out" some of the meanings. In general, Lynn begins at the beginning of the Bible, but meanings in even the earliest texts take him toward the New Testament. Let him lead you into some new associations between ideas; let this process open some windows to new understandings. Someone in the group/class might like to chart the key ideas in each Bible study and how Lynn makes the connections.

2. Become familiar with the whole study. This study covers a wide range of Biblical material. It moves from a beginning stage of responding to the God of creation, to the God who offers deliverance and salvation, to the God who invites us to receive the firstfruits of the Holy Spirit and begin to participate in what God is doing, to the God who invites us to maturity as even trouble enables us to experience and show God's adequacy, to a God who plans to make everything new.

Someone in your class or group may ask a question in an early session that is more properly a part of a later lesson. If you know all the material, you can accept the question but ask the person to bring it up again in the appropriate lesson. Make sure the question isn't lost.

3. Plan a participatory style of meeting where Bible and life intersect. For people to participate in the meeting, they need to know the material. If your group/class does not study in advance, find a good way to share the basic material and key concepts.

At Deep Run East, we decided the best way to help people get hold of the material was to have sermons on each Bible study with study questions highlighted. Teachers/discussion leaders can absorb the material and share it; this sharing must be brief so there is adequate time for discussion.

Summarizing and highlighting the material helps class members own it and bring it to mind. Then invite people to respond to what they perceive. Many of us hesitate to talk about firstfruits questions, particularly those related to money and lifestyle. Let the real questions surface. You may need to reshape the questions in the material to make them more useful in your class or group.

Don't be surprised if people at different stages in life talk about different things. How does God answer the anxiety of retired people who wonder if their resources will be adequate? What about young people who feel they will never accumulate enough to have a home? What about those who have a home and bills who wonder if the money earned will be adequate to pay?

Know the material well enough to point people to helpful areas. Be willing to talk about what it means to live by faith when the God in whom we have faith is one who has invested his only Son in us.

4. Expect this study to change lives. Sometimes we treat study as a purely academic exercise to gain information. Bible study is to help us meet God in Jesus; when it happens, that meeting is always so momentous that it is life changing! How do these materials invite us to experience more of what a firstfruits God is offering to us? What are the implications of being the representatives, the firstfruits in this world, of such a God? How shall we order our lives?

Provide opportunities for people to share ways they are reordering their lives because of the study; when people begin sharing their new commitments, your class/group will come alive with new vigor. Think about the ways you might share that will help others have faith to move. Can you teach by modeling?

5. Be alert for the need for additional experiences or resources. Are people needing help managing their money through better record keeping and decision making? Maybe *God's Managers*, a workbook by Ray and Lillian Bair to help Christians budget and manage their money, is needed.

Are people finding it difficult to resist the pressure

to spend too much without enough discretionary money left? The three-session video *In the Presence of Persuasion*, by Dan Hess, might help. Maybe you need counselors or small groups where these decisions are the subject matter. Bringing together a small group willing to talk about real questions often uncovers many additional resources. Don't be afraid to look for needed resources and experiences.

Firstfruits Living: Giving God Our Best is your invitation to adventure with God. May God bless you richly.

—*Arnold C. Roth*
Associate Mission Secretary,
Franconia Mennonite Conference

The Author

Lynn A. Miller was born in Peoria, Illinois, in 1941. He was the first son of parents who loved to travel and made frequent career changes. He grew up in eleven different towns in the United States, Japan, and France.

After leaving the family home in France as a high school junior, Lynn joined the Navy and spent the next six years on sea duty.

He married Linda (Pine) Miller, in 1965. After almost ten years of involvement in the Vietnam War, he left the service as a "rational pacifist," firmly convinced of the futility of using military force to solve the world's problems.

Now Lynn became a student at the University of Washington and an "overaged, underdeveloped flower child" and antiwar activist. Then he discovered some new roots in the welcome given to him by Linda's family and home church when they moved to eastern Ohio in 1970. Within the peaceful, servanthood faith of an Anabaptist fellowship, he experienced conversion and a sense of homecoming.

The next five years included two terms of voluntary service with the Brethren Disaster Service. He served first in Inverness, Mississippi, then in Brasstown, North Carolina.

After Lynn finished a B.S. degree in agriculture at Wilmington College (Ohio) in 1974, the family went from a farm in southern Ohio to Botswana as agricultural development workers with the Mennonite Central Committee.

Following three years in Botswana, Lynn became a staff chaplain in a local prison. That experience and his connection with the Mennonite work in criminal justice led Lynn and the family to Goshen Biblical Seminary (Elkhart, Indiana).

After receiving an M.Div. degree in 1985, Lynn was called by the South Union Mennonite Church in West Liberty, Ohio, to be their pastor. He was ordained there in 1987.

Linda is a registered nurse who does occasional relief duty in home health care nursing and inservice training. The Millers have two daughters, Lorraine, married to Darrell Nester, and Liana.